Sea Otters

Patricia Kendell

Raintree

Alligators Chimpanzees Dolphins Elephants
Giraffes Gorillas Grizzly Bears Hippos
Leopards Lions Orangutans Pandas Penguins
Polar Bears Rhinos Sea Otters Sharks Tigers

Published by Raintree, a division of Reed Elsevier, Inc.

Library of Congress Cataloging-in-Publication Data:

Kendell, Patricia.
  Sea otters / Patricia Kendell.
    p. cm. -- (In the wild)
Summary: Photographs and simple text introduce the behavior and habitat of sea otters.
Includes bibliographical references (p.   ).
  ISBN 0-7398-6639-7 (lib. bdg. : hardcover)
  1. Sea otter--Juvenile literature. [1. Sea otter. 2. Otters.] I.
Title. II. Series.
  QL737.C25 K395 2003
  599.769'5--dc21
                        2002152010

Printed in Hong Kong. Bound in the United States.

07 06 05 04 03
10 9 8 7 6 5 4 3 2 1

Photograph acknowledgments:
Bruce Coleman 17, 24 (Johnny Johnson);
Doc White 6, 7, 10, 13, 28, 29; FLPA 1 & 20 (Gerard Lacz),
9 (T Leeson/Sunset), 4, 23 (Mark Newman), 11, 14, 19 (Minden
Pictures); NHPA 18 (T Kitchin & V Hurst), 12, 22 (Norbert Wu);
OSF 21 (Richard Herrmann), 26 (Malcolm Penny/SAL),
15 (Frank Schneidermeyer), 25 (Kim Westerkov);
SPL 16 & 32 (Pat & Tom Leeson);
Still Pictures 27 (Chris Martin).

Contents

Where Sea Otters Live

Sea otters live in the Pacific Ocean off the coasts of the United States, Canada, and Russia.

A sea otter will spend most of its time in the sea.
But its close **relative**, the river otter (seen above),
often comes out onto the river bank.

Baby Sea Otters

A sea otter mother gives birth to one baby at a time. The **pup** is born in the water near the seashore.

The pup cannot swim at first, but its beautiful, fluffy
fur helps it to float. The sea otter mother often wraps
kelp around her pup to make sure the baby isn't
washed away.

Looking After the Pup

A sea otter mother carries the pup on her stomach to keep it safe and warm. She feeds her pup on milk that is rich in fat to help it grow quickly.

Sea otters do not have many enemies.
But a mother will try to protect her pup
from creatures such as this bald eagle.

Growing Up

By the time it is two months old, the pup has learned how to swim and dive underwater.

A mother sea otter teaches her pup where to find food and how to eat it. At six or seven months old, the pup can live on its own.

Family Life

Sea otters float closely together in the water.
A group of sea otters is called a raft.

Mother sea otters and their pups live together.
Groups of male otters live in groups, apart from
the females and pups.

Food

These colorful sea urchins are a favorite food of sea otters.

They eat many different sea creatures
including shellfish, like this crab.

Tools for Eating

Sea otters float on their backs and use their stomachs like a table. They break open the shellfish using a small rock.

This sea otter is using its teeth
to break open a mussel shell.

Keeping Warm

Sea otters have a lot of very thick fur
to keep them warm in the cold seawater.
They do not have a layer of fat like this seal.

Sea otters spend much time keeping their fur clean and fluffy. This sea otter is **grooming** her pup.

Swimming

Sea otters swim using their back feet, which act as flippers. They can stay underwater for several minutes at a time.

They do not often come on the land. When they do, they move awkwardly.

Resting

Sea otters sometimes pull **fronds** of kelp around themselves. This stops them from floating away in the moving water while they rest or sleep.

Sea otters sleep with their feet out of the water.
This helps them to stay warm.

Threats...

The sea otter has to **compete** with people who also like to eat shellfish. Fishermen are able to catch a lot of shellfish at one time.

Sometimes sea otters are shot because they take shellfish from **shellfish farms** like this one.

...and Dangers

The main danger for sea otters is oil **pollution**. If an otter's fur gets covered with oil, the otter gets cold and cannot swim well enough to find food.

Pollution from other dangerous chemicals
can make the sea otters and their **prey** sick.

Helping Sea Otters to Survive

People must try to prevent the sea from becoming polluted. This is important for all sea creatures.

If people learn more about what sea otters need,
then more of them will be able to survive in the future.

Further Information

Find out more about how we can help sea otters in the future.

ORGANIZATIONS TO CONTACT

World Wildlife Fund
1250 24th Street, N.W.
P.O. Box 97180
Washington, D.C. 20077-7180
http://www.wwf.org

Monterey Bay Aquarium
886 Cannery Row
Monterey Bay, CA 93940
http://www.mbayaq.org

BOOKS

Godkin, Celia. *Sea Otter Inlet*. Allston, MA: Fitzhenry & Whiteside Ltd., 2001.

Giles, Bridget. *Sea Otters*. Danbury, CT: Grolier Educational, 2001.

Kingston, George J. *The Exciting Adventures of Hydra and Muste Otter: Life in the Big Sea*. Los Gatos, CA: G Sharp Productions, 2001.

Meeker, Clare Hodgson. *Lootas, the Little Wave-Eater: An Orphaned Sea Otter's Story*. Seattle, WA: Sasquatch Books, 1999.

Glossary

WEBSITES

Most young children will need adult help when visiting websites. Those below have child-friendly pages to bookmark.

http://www.discovery.com/stories/nature/otters/otters.html
This site has stories about how sea otters are released back into the sea. Good for reading aloud to young children who can follow the story by looking at the pictures.

http://www.montereybayaquarium.org/cr/sorac.asp
This site has activities for children, as well as information about the sea otters at the Monterey Bay Aquarium.

compete – (kum-PEET) to try to win against someone.

fronds – (frondz) bits of seaweed that wave about in the water.

grooming – (GROOM-ing) cleaning the coat of an animal.

kelp – (kelp) a type of seaweed.

pollution – (poh-LOO-shun) when water or air becomes filled with poisons.

prey – (pray) an animal hunted and eaten by another animal.

pup – (pup) a baby sea otter.

relative – (REL-uh-tivz) an animal in the same family.

shellfish farm – (shell-fish farm) places in the sea where people raise shellfish.

Index

32